Box Turtle

Children Book of Fun Facts & Amazing Photos on Animals in Nature - A Wonderful Box Turtle Book for Kids aged 3-7

By

Ina Felix

Hello, I am a box turtle.

I have a brown shell that I call my home.

My shell can have pretty patterns.

I live in North America.

I like to be with other turtles.

I love to eat berries, flowers, and small insects.

I hide in my shell when I get scared. So if you want me to be your friend, please be gentle and kind to me.

I can live for more than 80 years.

I have no teeth, but I like to bite.

I like to move slowly. Forgive me if you want me to run along with you, but I just cannot run because of my hard, heavy shell and short legs.

I like to stay on the land.

My turtle babies are hatched from my eggs.

I can lay three to eight eggs.

My eggs take three months to hatch.

I have a cute little tail.

I like to sleep in the winter.

I find ways to cool down, especially when it gets too hot.

I like to live near the water.

My shell can heal, if I get hurt.

I like it when it rains.

I hope you had fun learning about my family.

Thank you.

CPSIA information can be obtained
at www.ICGtesting.com
Printed in the USA
LVHW062325041118
595953LV00004B/27/P